KEEP THIS FOREVER

KEEP THIS FOREVER

MARK HALLIDAY

POEMS

TUPELO PRESS

COPYRIGHT

Tupelo Press
PO Box 539, Dorset, Vermont 05251
www.tupelopress.org

COVER AND TEXT DESIGN BY HOWARD KLEIN

Front cover photos courtesy of the author.

Tupelo Press is an award-winning independent literary press that publishes fine fiction, non-fiction and poetry in books that are as much a joy to hold as they are to read. Tupelo Press is a registered 501(c)3 non-profit organization and relies on donations to carry out its mission of publishing extraordinary works of literature that may be outside the realm of large commercial publishers.

ACKNOWLEDGMENTS

The following poems (or earlier versions of them) appeared in journals, as follows:

"Chicken Salad" in *The Gettysburg Review*
"Last Touch" in *The Southern Review*
"Milt and Sally" in *The Hopkins Review*
"Clearing the Apartment" in *Hunger Mountain*
"Walking the Ashes" in *Crab Orchard Review*
"Dreamhooked" in *TriQuarterly*
"A Night in 2029" in *Agni Online*
"Each Minute" in *The Southern Review*
"Do It Deftly" in *Fugue*
"Google Me Soon" in *Crazyhorse*
"Sternly Departing" in *Poetry*
"Not Exactly Woody Guthrie" in *Fugue*
"Special Heads" in *TriQuarterly*
"Confession to Mary" in *Willow Springs*
"Shmedlo Talk" in *The Missouri Review*
"Vim" in *Green Mountains Review*
"Muck-Clump" in *TriQuarterly*
"Warren" in *Indiana Review*
"Dorie Off to Atlanta" in *The Gettysburg Review*
"Tim Off to Charlotte" in *The Missouri Review*
"Plot Notes" in *Pool*
"Not That Great of an Evening" in *The Gettysburg Review*
"Three Flaws" in *Crazyhorse*
"To You in 2052" in *Michigan Quarterly Review*
"Down Here" in *The Journal*
"Another Point" in *Alaska Quarterly Review*
"Julie at the Reading" in *Crazyhorse*
"Enchanted Field" in *Mississippi Review*
"Ask Wendy Wisdom" in *The Hopkins Review*
"South of Morgantown" in *Shade*
"Guidebook Embarrassment" in *Columbia Poetry Review*
"Way Way Up There" in *The Southern Review*

"Way Way Up There" borrows a line and a half from Richard Wilbur's translation of "Compass" by Jorge Luis Borges.

Let others glut on the extorted praise
Of vulgar breath; trust thou to after days:
Thy laboured works shall live, when time devours
The abortive offspring of their hasty hours.
— *Thomas Carew*

Even I, while humble zeal
Makes fancy a sad truth indite,
Insensible away do steal;
And when I'm lost in death's cold night,
Who will remember, now I write?
— *William Habington*

CONTENTS

WALKER

Milt in his last month as a sentient being
pushing his walker along the narrow bumpy
dark blue corridor toward the bathroom
fighting his way for the sake of some
sense of dignity still not quite demolished
though it is so thin and transparent nearly as air;
he pauses to breathe and then lifts the walker just enough
to angle it past the buxom terra cotta torso
of the young young woman always out there ahead

CHICKEN SALAD

Everybody's father dies.
When it happens to someone else, I send a note of sympathy
or at least an e-mail. It's certainly worth the bother.
But when my father died, it was *my father.*

*

Three hours before he died
my father felt he should have an answer
when I asked what he might like to eat.
He remembered a kind of chicken salad he liked
weeks ago when living was more possible
and he said "Maybe that chicken salad"
but because of the blood in his mouth
and because of his shortness of breath
he had to say it several times before I understood.
So I went out and bought a container of chicken salad,
grateful for the illusion of helping,
but when I brought it back to the apartment
my father studied it for thirty seconds
and set it aside on the bed. I wasn't ready
to know what the eyes of the nurse at the Hospice
had tried to tell me before dawn, so I said
"Don't you want your chicken salad, Daddy?"
He glanced at it from a distance of many miles—
little tub of chicken salad down on the planet of
slaughtered birds and mastication, digestion, excretion—
and murmured "Maybe later." He was in
the final austerity
which I was too frazzled to quite recognize
but ever since his death I see with stony clarity

the solitary dignity of
the totality of his knowing
how far beyond the pleasure of chicken salad
he had gone already and would go.

＊

Everybody's father dies; but
when my father died, it was my father.

SKEIN

At the moment when my father died
I was in the next room
on the phone talking to my wife
five hundred miles away.
We had so much to say.
With animation we spoke of life:
next week, next month—
a skein of possibilities in play.
I talked with unusual briskness
and sharp enunciation because
I knew I must be a vigorous adult
with a major problem just one room away.
Dimly hearing all that, my father
rested his hands on the cool sheet
and felt there wasn't enough reason to stay.

LAST TOUCH

He lay there propped up on his bed
deathmasked

When I leaned down and kissed his forehead
it was not exactly that I felt a warm wish to kiss him

it was more that I needed a gesture
an outward sign of farewell
Maybe I knew that later I would need to remember
that I leaned down and kissed his forehead

I was not full of grief
though grief was quietly building its embassy
far downtown in my head

I was in awe of my own astonishment
transfixed by the loud silence of the blatancy of
my pure inadequacy in the encounter
but I kissed his cool forehead
like someone saying Goodbye full of feeling
to help myself feel it later
in the icicle moments of sudden reality.

IT WAS NOT HIM

It was not him in the black bag.
It was not him
in the black bag.
It was
not him—

because if it
had been him
I would never have allowed
the two guys from Crestwood Memorial,
the wiry pale one and the plump sweaty one
to roll him into the huge black fake-leather bag and
zip it up and carry him (pretending not to strain)
(he was a big man) (had been) past the blue couch
and the tiny dirty kitchen and angle him—
angle it through the doorway to the landing
where I held open the elevator door with one hand
while gripping his black cat Cleo in my other hand
so she wouldn't follow him into the elevator—

of course I would never have permitted any of that
if it had been him in the black bag
but it
was not him
and so all this did occur
and I stood with Cleo in the silence of the apartment
while the black bag journeyed jostling away south down Manhattan.

MILT AND SALLY

Twenty days after my father died I threw away
all the letters between him and Sally Pierce
written in the mid-Thirties—
all that yearning and uncertainty, admiration and doubt—
the love of Milt and Sally;
she was the one he didn't marry
and in sixty-some further years he didn't forget...
Sally died young. Milt died very old.
Twenty days later I swam down into the files

and couldn't keep everything. Couldn't keep. Everything.

So I chucked the Sally letters, unread,
because I was not God.
God would be the Omnivorous Reader.
God might not *see* the little sparrow's fall
but if the sparrow or its mate wrote an account of it—
My Lamentable Fall From the Sky—
God would read every page;
Our Lord would savor every sentence.
And never put it back on the shelf!

My father was quite sure God didn't exist
and for most of his life he felt sure this was
a good thing, or at least extremely acceptable.
In his last two years I think he felt more
a sad irritation or that God's nonexistence is (as he would say)
a hell of a note.

Not being God, I tossed the entire yellowed bundle
and a wraith, or invisible powder of old paper,

rose from the black bag to watch me
from the ceiling of the littered posthumous apartment.
Surely the wraith could see my predicament.
Not being God, I had to be Nature.

*

GOD'S READING NOTES

Milt was confused by too many desires,
and more romantic than he knew.
Sally was more cautious than her flamboyance implied,
and less romantic than she believed.
Milt and Sally—like their friends,
a bit overcomplicated for this green and blooded world,
but a damned good read.

CLEARING THE APARTMENT

It's funny how it is—I mean,
on the one hand, when he dies it's a big deal,
it's a project I mean it's a *major* hassle—

you have to go through his files, he has hundreds of files,
you make piles like blocks of an igloo around you
but the piles keep falling sideways, what to throw out,
what to keep, keep this and this because his personality is reflected
but not so much in this, better throw out more, it's getting late,
what about the photos, there must be a thousand photos—
you can't keep them all, that would be crazy, oh
here's another box of letters, these are from 1937 and 1938
when people had HEARTS and MINDS just like you and me
god damn it oh god here's *another* box of letters
and this envelope holds more photos—these faces:
modestly optimistic, or sweetly cheerful

and here is his drawer full of "useful things"
many of which you can't even identify
and here in another drawer what's this?
This is eight versions of the play he wrote
in the early Seventies about Thomas Jefferson, each version meant
something—keep the last version—it's really late now
and your eyes are the size of silver dollars with crazed wakefulness
and you find in the closet a box of color slides, hold a few
up to the light: that's the bicycle trip in 1964...
How much does it mean? How much? How much?

Now for his kitchen: this oatmeal is probably five years old
and these cans of chicken soup are ancient
and you stand there wondering what to feel for those poor
chickens of a lost decade
but decisions have to be made

and nobody wants this old chipped china…
Keep the blue dish his beloved gave him in 1936
because he kept it and you don't want to imagine him
watching when you throw it away
but everything else goes in black plastic bags, you need
more black bags—

what about this toy Ford auto it must date from 1920 when he was seven
do you keep it? I don't think so—it doesn't roll—
bring more black bags—Christ what a hassle I mean
what an ordeal, it's big—

on the other hand, now four days have passed, now it's the fifth day
and the trash truck has come and gone
and the boxes are in the station wagon,
you sweep the floor, it's swept,
the broom leans in the corner very dry and quiet,
very competent yet modest,
you pick up a dime from the closet,
the place is empty. You're done.

WALKING THE ASHES

When I picked up my father's ashes
at Crestwood Memorial Chapel downtown
the box was astoundingly heavy
just as everyone always says about human ashes
and besides he was a big man—but still

I wanted to walk with him for a while—
to see how it felt to walk with his ashes
through streets he walked so vigorously in the Thirties,
the noisy exciting Thirties which were the present then

so we set out in the sunshine.
A restaurant on the corner of Spring and Mott
had Specials on a sidewalk chalkboard
and the top Special was Salmon Affumicato with Vodka Cream
and I said "That sounds good"
but the ashes said "Maybe a little too fancy."

My father liked his pleasures bold and clear and decisive;
he used to say the way to throw a good party was to roast
a big ham and put it on the table with a sharp knife
and let everybody just hack off chunks

and he made me feel sort of effete at times;
but he also inspired me to love my own opinions.
The sun blazed and my arms began to hurt
but we kept walking for at least thirty blocks, comparing notes;

I kept suggesting that the day was bright with meaning
but the ashes suspected it was all absurdly blank,
all drained of something grand that Benny Goodman once expressed.

We agreed in admiration of certain women on their lunch hour,
but the ashes muttered something about beauty being
an intolerable trick in a world that turns you eighty-nine years old.

"Well, Daddy, I'm still on my feet" I said
but it was hot and my arms did hurt so I hailed a cab.

The ashes on the back seat of the cab were quiet
and I was quiet, we let New York stream past the windows,
let it go, because even the most vigorous walkers
with the most emphatic opinions
will eventually need a break from the world.

DREAMHOOKED

In a blue notebook in maybe 1983
I drafted an Ode to Sexual Fantasy
which probably was quite bad because too simple and obvious
and much less merry and incisive than I imagined;
well, I must have known it wasn't great
since I let it stay in the notebook
and left the notebook in a drawer in my father's house in Vermont—

I don't think I wanted him to see it
but I guess he probably did on some dull Saturday
when he was trying to clear the old files and drawers and shelves—

I feel queasy thinking of him reading my Ode to Sexual Fantasy—
him in his seventies, me in my thirties—
my father standing there in the dusty quiet house
reading my lines about how sexual fantasy helps keep us alive—
stirring the embers—sustaining the dream-hope for Shangri-La;

surely I had two or three metaphors not utterly flaccid?—
And I hope the poem included also an awareness
that sexual fantasy may also be part of what ages and kills us,
because always there arrives the moment of realizing
how idiotically repetitious the fantasies are—
bosoms bottom boom bosoms bottom boom—
and how pathetically distant from what will happen
for the dreamhooked boy of thirty-eight, or seventy-three...

I do hope that's all there in the Ode
because it would imply I wasn't just being sheerly stupidly ordinary
when I wrote it—so my father reading it
alone in the dusty Vermont house
would see that his son was not just stupidly ordinary—

but then also he would feel sad, sad to be at the mercy of the images—
Jane Russell, Marilyn Monroe, Raquel Welch,
a certain secretary in 1974,
the fabulous warm unreachable weighty passionating shapes—
sad to be reminded that he still had not escaped;
and sad to see how garishly and helplessly his son had inherited the
dreamhook;

so I'm afraid my failed poem may have added one more shade
to the layered sadness of being seventy-three or seventy-eight
one long Saturday alone in Vermont in a jumbled house.

He kept himself alive, though,
not without some gladness till he was eighty-nine,
nourished as well as ravaged by irresistible wishing.

And if at the age of sixty I find that blue notebook
in an old file or box there will be
the shadow of a tremor of embarrassment
and a distant low pulsing of sadness
as if a low note were softly played
several times on a piano downstairs;

nourished but also ravaged we are
by irresistible failures of representing
—representing because
the actual breathing talking perceptive woman is *much* too complicated;

and I'll keep the notebook in a pile of old things
that represent me—the acorn, Daddy, not too far from the tree—

and just for a minute, that night,
a ghost of Maggie or Liz or Patty or Tracy will visit me, radiant—

LES MORTS

Les morts vont vite uh huh you can say that again
The dead go quickly
Lay morh vonh veet

My aunt Dorothy had a gentleness in her blue eyes
My aunt Lois had in her blue eyes an expectation of fun
They were my father's sisters; he was alive when I started
writing this in a notebook

Lay morh vonh veet
Not just that they go
but that their being gone itself has a clipped decisiveness
in the tingly sunshine

Kenneth Fearing's "Requiem" is great
I say so but Fearing doesn't listen

Lisa W brought tangerines up to the roof
and we watched the traffic below
afraid of enough but not of time—

thirty years later she suddenly died in California
leaving a family I never met
I think of her once or twice a month maybe

on a huge steady ship

Lay morh vonh veet
My father's friend Bob Weeks loved Stephen Crane
and he could tell you why in such a way that you loved
every word because you wanted to love like that
then years *daze anh* then prostate cancer and gone

Everyone is on a huge steady ship

conturbat me but really not most minutes
walking to class walking to the post office

Dickinson's "What care the Dead, for Chanticleer—"
I can "teach" it rather seriously without quite
glimpsing her at that upstairs window

vonh veet

The e-mail came about Kenneth Koch's death
and an hour later as we shopped at the thriving market
we tried to see the *calamari* and *branzini* and *aragoste* and *gamberetti*
with his kind of enthusiasm—*pecorino, caprino, fiore sardo,*
pomodori, zucchini, everything freshly sure we would forget

What can we do we can't stumble around
remembering them all day—
they should visit us if they want to be kept
well they do they do visit but so briefly,
without planning, without warning, so skittish

Norman!—
Norman, we got our skis and poles from the rack outside the lodge
and continued some thread of talk that began over cocoa inside
and you quoted Yeats asking "what if excess of love
Bewildered them till they died?"
I was maybe twenty-one, you were maybe fifty-five.
Ten or fifteen years later I'd be able to think harder
about whether Yeats had the right true words there
but what you gave me, Norman—
we were just middle-classy vacationers on a two-family ski trip
gawky in our puffy jackets and fat mittens but also
we were the ones on Okemo Mountain
loving word-magic with a fine excessiveness

which glistened like new snow and made us terrific.

Yet I think of Norman so seldom and almost never
open his books. Days are made of hours—*vonh veet*—
books—new books—buy some new books—
bought three yesterday—out comes the credit card—
new books crisp new books not part of
any disappointment or fading: buy two more today!

Two years before Gerry died at age forty,
on our last evening with him I made him discuss elegy—
my obsession at the time—the relation between elegy and detail;
he surprised me by taking it more seriously than I was taking it;
he said "Commemoration is actually rather complicated—
one doesn't want to become merely someone's nifty phrases."
Lay morh vonh veet
you can say that again

Everyone is on a huge steady ship
far out on such a great ocean you can hardly tell
the engines are churning
and when someone falls from the deck
the splash is so brief
and if you try to watch the spot where the splash happened
quickly quickly it is far back there and fluxed over
in the gray green undulation far back and now
indistinguishable

Okay so you have to be gone those of you who have gone
we can't ride that inkdark pony into the heart of night not yet

you have to ride that trail without us
brushing past the black thick leaves on either side
farther and farther without seeing anything
miles and cool black miles without caring or hurting at all

while we can live somewhat inflected by what you were.

A NIGHT IN 2029

I could live to be eighty and one night in 2029
stand leaning on the table in my kitchen
hit suddenly with a vision of the kitchen at 64 Elmgrove
one night in 1973 where I sat with Laird Holby
and he read aloud a passage from *Howards End*—

I could look for that passage and not be sure
but it said something about music and I think implied
a way to live for the glory of spirit without becoming absurd—

hit with that vision in 2029 I stand eighty years old
feeling I might wobble and fall and break my arm or hip
not because of ordinary weakness but because of suddenly knowing
that except for being an old man I am still nothing
but that young guy with wild hair, listening thoughtfully to Laird.

I could live to be eighty and I guess I have to wish for that
but I'm afraid of the minute in 2029
when I wobble in the sudden wind that blows
down the long shady corridor from 1973
when I suspected the reward for listening thoughtfully would be
to always have a delicious great chance to be
the beautiful understander
for whom everything including time makes good sense.

EACH MINUTE

The night my friend phoned from the Cancer Center in Houston
to tell me he'd been diagnosed with leukemia,
the news colored my thoughts and sub-thoughts.
Among them were these nine:

* He must have done something wrong; the world is very stern.

* He didn't do anything wrong—the world is insane!

* A spot on my neck seems sore—maybe I have a terrible disease,
   that would be grotesquely unfair because I have so much to do!

* Get my files in order, alphabetize, make everything clear,
   revise everything, label the boxes, vacuum the floor around the file
   cabinets and wipe the cobwebs from the windowsill…

* Each minute while I do *anything*—I go across 55th Street
   to pick up the Japanese take-out,
   I walk to 63rd Street to see the movie "Sexy Beast"
   or I buy Gourmet Fish Feast for my father's cat—
   my friend lies in that hospital bed anticipating chemotherapy
   and the failure of chemotherapy each minute—each minute—

* To be serious is very tiring.

* But it can also be rather calming, and makes me kind of noble.

* But I will forget to be serious. I will forget, and then I will deserve
   whatever punishment there is for forgetting—if there is a punishment.

* Instead of *being* so damned serious I want thirty more years
   to worry about what it means and doesn't mean.

DO IT DEFTLY

Rain steady down upon the yard and woodpile,
the Japanese maples and decrepit picnic table,
uncountably small droplets down and down—

a cardinal flies off into the dripping grove—
puddles vibrate steadily on the gray plastic chairs;
the total pallor of rain sky creates
a reflective sheen on the deck's weathered boards

and the spirit calms into stilled acceptance
of loss and eventual death.

                         Ah, acceptance—

forty-five seconds later at the rainspotted window
you're planning to tell
someone—or better yet everyone—
how ineffable your moment was. Do it deftly
and we'll give you a prize
long before your last ride to the hospital.

NO STRATEGY

There was no way to keep it
when I ran to meet Cathy
at the statue of Marcus Aurelius
five minutes late as usual
in bounteous lavish spring sun
there was no way to keep
Cathy with her sunglasses and her dark straight hair
and her eyes skeptical and optimistic at once
and the entire old campus built specially for us
and possibility so infinite it had to be comic

—there was no method
there was no available strategy
it's not as if we could have kept it all
if only we were smarter. . .
Lightly we kissed and lightly walked and talked
of books in which we'd read only twenty pages
the days were long but fast
we had to stop the Vietnam War
and grow up but first
head for the Ivy Room
for ice cream with Rich and Liz.

GOOGLE ME SOON

From the way you barely glance at me downtown
I sense you guess I'm not much but this is a mistake.
I have traveled through 13 tunnels and over 67 bridges
to Honey Island. Details are available. My high baritone goes
from G clear to B, I do a Cockney accent and martial arts,
I have walked out on the pier straight into the Devil's Throat
and I have danced for the goddess Iemanja.
Have you danced for the goddess Iemanja?
I doubt that you have. Bev Swain in Sydney loves my work by the way
like when I created Detective Ryan Legrand
and sent him deep into what I call Antonioni Land. That was my idea.
As the latest member of the Derby Ducks
my passion is high-performance cars and I can go EXTREMELY
fast. When Gemma sees me clock-tock the flag-box *she* knows
why I've been often called the Kelso Laddie. That's
the Kelso Laddie. But who am I talking to? You
don't even know Gemma, do you? I didn't think so.
Got any color shots of Ilho do Mel? You should be so lucky!
Maybe it's time for you to practice some respect?
I have drunk submarinos with Norwegian blondes whose hair is
like silk. Silk! Silk! Hey wait—wait a minute I'm not—

did I mention my high baritone goes clear to B?
You and I, we could have a connection, a link,
you could send me your questions about wine coolers and corkscrews
and I would answer in full. Listen,
shall I put you in touch with Bev Swain in Sydney? Listen,
don't underestimate: in the edifice of my spirit
there are live performers poised at every window!
All they need is for you to look up from the heartless traffic.

STERNLY DEPARTING

Nobody seemed to notice me for three days in San Diego
as if I were less significant than a spindly palm tree
yet when my plane took off from the airport
at that moment all over San Diego people paused
and glanced into some crystal of absence;
the plane's wheels lifted unequivocally from the runway
and San Diego was left with a diminished portion of the possible

and in particular several thousand quite healthy women
in their twenties and thirties (okay and early forties)
felt a sudden shiver and fearfully touched their hair
as my plane rose sternly into the blue
of the tremendous Unavailable, so gone and so debonair.

NOT EXACTLY WOODY GUTHRIE

As I lugged my luggage past the airport bar
I angled my neck to peer between drinkers
to see whether the field goal was good
in whatever game it was
because those people cared apparently
and I wanted for a second not to be too different.

*

Okay but also wanted to reap the benefit for a few seconds
of an image of successful performance in a ritualized activity
where skill earns unerasable points
and the swarming helmeted deniers can't quite reach you.

SPECIAL HEADS

This one loves W. G. Sebald, and that one loves Joseph Cornell.
This one adores Preston Sturges, and that one devours Ruth Rendell.
Each one of them carries a special head
up on his or her shoulders, till she/he be dead.
To prefer, and opine, each one has a right
for this is America, where each soul shines bright.
Oh frum frum boojwacka frum—
I have my own views, but am feeling so glum.

I love doo wop, I do do do,
it's something to me though it's not much to you—
why should you worry what looms large to me
or why I admire Buñuel's *Discreet Charm of the Bourgeoisie?*
Da dink da da dink da da dink da da dink:
if I keep a deft rhythm I might make you think
you've encountered a Witty New Voice on the Scene
da da dink da da dink, but how long could I preen—
I love *The Crying of Lot Forty-neen*

and could tell you why with charming enthusiasm
if you were very ready to be charmed
but I suspect you come to the encounter armed
with your own identity-propping choices.
America, land of the too-many voices—

Why too many, you ask, why not embrace all?
La ba noof la ba noof and we're off to the mall,
everybody likes something, everybody's a shopper,
you can write the latest poem about Edward Hopper...
My point is, the noise—

actually my point is that when you love
the isolated figure in the painting of the late-night diner

the pain of your love is the hard-to-repress understanding
that the profoundly respectful rescuing eyes of the painter
do *not* gaze from across the street outside
all the real diners, late, late on Friday night.
And my point is that when you come bopping to tell us
how much you love Fragonard or the Big Bopper
you want to be loved for your precious admiring

and you *are* rather lovely at the moment when your caring
is truly focused and truly intense (even if you're just describing
Allen Iverson as he incredibly outwits and outhustles
all five of the New York Knicks and creates
a suddenly fresh sense of what one person still might do
in a world of violent towering alien forces)
but we're about to be distracted, any second now,
by some other beauty or mere flurry of Chantilly Lace,
it's just about to happen
before you even utter your last—

CONFESSION TO MARY

Mary! When I caught your eye across two tables of canapés
and failed to smile at you and then turned away
to focus on apple slices smeared with blue cheese, Mary!
I was a fool! Because the cheese and fruit were finite

whereas you were of infinity, Mary, you
with such a wild lonesome light in your eyes
and your way of speaking too loudly in order to cut through
the smog of cultured politesse—and I love

the way you create a burlesque of decadence
just in how you shake the ice in your glass—
but Mary! I was afraid you might pull me into
such a peculiar conversation I might miss my chance

to dramatize my wit for the rosy applause of
those two strapless daughters of the famous architect
but Mary I am an ass—choosing the ersatz immortality
of imaginary simplistic Don Juaning when I could be

fathoming the unknowable deeps of your teak-brown eyes
oh Mary—ride back toward me on your transparent llama
across the black dunes of my smallheaded shallowosity
and splash me with the chill high sarcasm of your differentness!

SHMEDLO TALK

Did you hear about Clodia and Valerius?

I heard something.

What did you hear?

You tell me first.

Well, they were drinking wine under the fig tree last night

and, you know, they were kind of leaning toward each other.

They were leaning?

Yeah.

Are we talking about shmedlo?

Whoa, wait, I didn't mean shmedlo.

You didn't?

Well—not yet.

Did you hear what Fedelta said about Lyubka and Froim?

Well, Zeno mentioned something.

Zeno! That's ironic. I mean, considering the way he and Augusta carry on.

Carry on? I heard they were smordling at the New Year's party.

Yeah but who did you hear it from? Cybele?

Yeah.

Well, consider the source.

Okay, but still. I can imagine them having excellent shmedlo.

Ewww, I don't want to think about it.

You'd rather think about medieval churches?

By the way, what's the story on Lepida and Ahenobarbus?

Fedelta says they've crossed the Rubicon.

Really? How do we know?

Well, Fedelta saw them talking in the garden.

Talking in the garden? What does that prove?

Talking like "privately." Fedelta said the vibes were weird.

When Pylades walked over to them they like immediately changed the subject.

Well, maybe the subject was Pylades.

Anyway, if they do it—

Who? Lepida and Ahenobarbus?

No, Lyubka and Froim. If they do it, I would just say it's about time.

I mean they've been wanting to since October.

What do you mean "if" they do it?

Where do you think they go when they play "tennis"?

Well, I don't think it's actual shmedlo.

I think it's just furlbeesking.

Yeah—with maybe a little smordling on the side.

Oh, smordling—that's Valerius's specialty.

Valerius is like addicted to smordling,

it's like the arrabiata sauce on his penne.

On his what?

So you think with Clodia it's just smordling

and not shmedlo?

Unfortunately.

Unfortunately?

Yeah. To tell the truth, I'm not sure there's *any* shmedlo around here.

Oh come on.

I'm serious. I think Cybele and Attis might be

the only ones who've had shmedlo since Christmas.

Get out of here!

Well, I do sometimes suspect there's a lot more *talk* about shmedlo

than actual shmedlo.

That's sort of sad.

Well, shmedlo does tend to cause trouble, sooner or later.

I'm getting depressed.

But wait, did you hear about Ahenobarbus and Augusta?

Augusta? Are you kidding?

Kidding? I couldn't sleep last night,

I kept thinking about how miserable Lepida must be.

Why do you care so much about Lepida?

What? Well, I'm just a caring person, and I sympathize,

she must be so unhappy.

Maybe you kind of over-identify with her,

maybe you're a lonely person so you over-identify

with anyone who gets left alone.

Thanks for your insight, doctor.

Alone! Lepida? I thought she crossed the Rubicon with Ahenobarbus.

That's if you believe Fedelta.

Well, frankly I hope it's true. And I hope it happens with Lyubka and Froim.

And when I heard about Clodia and Valerius I thought

"Thank God somebody around here sees the moon as a dish of hot
                transcendence

and the stars as a foretaste of possible ecstasy."

How many limoncellos have you had?

I just don't want to think shmedlo is only an idea.

Well, there's always Cybele and Attis.

Maybe or maybe not. How often do you think they really have shmedlo?

Once in the Eighties, once in the Nineties.

I'm getting depressed again.

But why is shmedlo so important? Seriously, why do we worry about it
                all the time?

Oh come on.

Basically it's just a biological urge. Nature drives us toward shmedlo.

We exaggerate its spiritual significance.

More can happen in certain moments of eye contact

than in a whole night of shmedlo.

Wow, you must have had some bad shmedlo;

or some great eye contact.

Anyway, you wouldn't be such a philosopher

if your own partner was the one out there doing it.

You're speaking hypothetically, right?

Hey, can we talk about art or something?

Sure. But after that, tell me the rest about Lepida and Ahenobarbus.

We feel shmedlo is a chance to break through

the bubble of solitude *and* the banality of mortality,

both at once. That's why we can't stop talking about it.

Yeah, well—if we're right then I hope

we all get a lot of it before we're gone.

VIM

Some people just seem to exist, as opposed to *live*,
in a foggy drift. I am so glad that's not me!

I am certainly so glad I have such thumping
zest for life. The way I dig into life
like a bowl of hot Texas chili with sour cream
and shredded sharp cheddar—I'm so glad

I have such a pulsing intuitive grasp
of how short and precious life is
and how we are impassioned clay
and each incredible *diem* is there to be *carped*

so therefore I skim speedingly over the waters of life
alert to every flick of fin
and super-ready to jab my osprey talons into
the flesh of whatever sensation swims my way
not fretting for a second about any other plump fish in the sea

and so for example when I see young couples
groobling moistly at each other's burger-fed gamoofs
I certainly don't waste my time with any type of envy,
I'm just like Yeah you kids go for it!—
Meanwhile I am going to listen to *Let It Bleed* LOUD
and totally rock out with all my teeth bared!
I figure I am at least as alive as Little Richard was in 1958
and it's such a kick!

Does it get tiring?
                    Well, sure, occasionally,
but who cares? I *embrace* the fatigue,
I KISS it till it flips and becomes defiantly voracious vim

and when I read that line in Wallace Stevens
"being part is an exertion that declines"
I'm like What in heck is that old guy talking about?

MUCK-CLUMP

My wife was being too *busy* around the kitchen one morning
I think to give herself the sense of being on top of things
and when I poured a bowl of Shredded Wheat Spoonfuls for Devon
my wife bustled over and said "Oh Devon likes to have more cereal
  than that"
so she poured more Spoonfuls on top of the considerable number I
  had poured.
This griped me because now it was as if I hadn't given Devon her breakfast
because it might as well have been my wife who did it all
which would imply that I wasn't really making a contribution,
as if I were just a log of driftwood on the sand of time
while everyone else built the boats and caught the fish
and made the whole human drama fare forward against the void.

So I watched Devon pour a lot of milk on her Shredded Spoonfuls
and I figured she would hardly eat half of them
and when she went out to the schoolbus there would be
this awful soggy mass of decomposing cereal left behind
which would resemble the way I often see myself
so I figured then I could show the bowl to my wife
and I'd say "Do you think Devon got enough cereal?"
and the moment of sarcasm would be exquisite.
While Devon ate Spoonfuls I tied her shoes—I did accomplish that—
and I imagined how I would say it with measured irony
that would sting slightly but also come across as witty:
"Do you think Devon got enough cereal?"—I would say it
and then vigorously dump the sodden milky muck-clump into the trash.
It would be a moment in which I would be quite noticeably
on top of things... Then the bus came
and Devon hoisted her backpack and hurried outside, calling Goodbye,

and I saw with astonishment that her cereal bowl was empty.
How was I going to deal with this? It wouldn't be fair

to be angry at Devon for her unreasonable appetite; but
I could possibly complain about my wife's failure to provide
a more balanced breakfast for our daughter—but I sensed
that this challenge would backfire because my wife is the one
who really does think about nutrition and besides there were, actually,
some strawberries on Devon's placemat.
So I decided to rise above the entire episode, to be large-minded,
to wash a few dishes nonchalantly and read the newspaper
and make an insightful remark about something in the news.
Awareness of a larger world, after all, is
a central part of being mature, which is
something I want to believe I am—
when you see some old chunk of driftwood on the beach
you might say "That looks so calm, so peaceful"
or you might say "That is so dry and dead"
but you don't say "That is really mature."

WARREN

I think I need a card to operate the printer. I can walk
to the front desk and ask about a card. There's no rush.
Right foot, left foot. The key thing is to keep it together because
if I don't—the edge is close by. I am clean and I am standing
straight up and I walk across this long library carpet
in a straight line. Keeping it together. Nancy
will not let me see Sonya unless I get it all together.
What's this in my pocket—it's the application form
from Taco Bell. That's how far down—
but pride is not the thing needed. Or not the wrong type of pride.
Starting it all over. Starting up. But if the panic comes—

when the panic comes, do I let it come?
The question itself is not clear. The pronoun "I" is
confusing in itself. But the haircut I have is a neat haircut
and this little mustache is a neat touch. And when I phone Nancy
there is not going to be any shouting whatsoever
and not any crying whatsoever. Because—Sonya—
she's my daughter. And it doesn't get more important than that.
Because if that's not important, then—
"we won't go there." My daughter.
That's—man, if you forget that, you're just gone.
And I did decide to stick around on earth.
And I am not moving to Arizona because then
I cannot swear I would come back to see Sonya.
And she is my daughter! So I am still in this town,
same town where she lives

and I am writing *Lost Prince of Planet Zarvo*
each day in the library while I keep
everything together.

DORIE OFF TO ATLANTA

Jen? Hi, it's Dorie. I'm on the bus to La Guardia. … Atlanta.
What? … Maybe. I'm not really sure. I mean his schedule is so whacked,
y'know? … But anyway, I was telling you about Marcie. Yeah. So
I said to her, I said Marcie, this one seems different, y'know?
I said the last few guys you've dated—from what you've told me—
I mean frankly—… Yeah. I said Marcie, they might be
like very charming, y'know, and with great jobs, but frankly—
what it comes down to is Let's hit the bed,
and in the morning Thanks for the excellent coffee. Y'know?
But this guy—… What? It's Jason. Yeah.
So I said Marcie, from what you've said, Jason sounds different—
and from what Bob said about him also. … Bob knows him
from some project last fall. So I said Marcie, you've had, what,
two coffees, two lunches and a *dinner* and he still hasn't—…
No, Bob says he's definitely straight. …
I think there was a divorce like six years ago or something. But my—
What? … That's right, yeah, I did. At Nathan's party after some show.
… Yeah, "The Duchess of Malfi," I forgot I told you. What? …
Only for five minutes—one cigarette, y'know? … Kind of low-key,
like thoughtful. But my point is—… Yeah, exactly! So I said
Marcie, this is a guy who understands, y'know,
that bed is like *part* of something, y'know?
Like it's not the big *objective* for godsake. It's like an *aspect*—
What? … Exactly—it's an expression of something much more—
yes!—it's like Can we be companions in *life*, y'know?
So I said Marcie, for godsake—if you don't give this guy
like a serious chance, somebody else—y'know? … Right,
I mean let's face it—not that I… What? Yeah, it's like reality is
what actually happens! … Jen?
I'm losing you here—am I breaking up?
Jen, I'll call you from the airport—Okay bye.

TIM OFF TO CHARLOTTE

Christine, Tim here. Just to let you know I've touched base with
  Herman Schmitt
He's on board. It's a go
Whatever you can pull together will be helpful
Jim, this is Tim McCurdy, just getting back to you about the
  Big Boys project
Not sure if your people are up to date on this
Just to be sure we all shoot in the same direction
Christine, something I didn't mention
The reason Herman Schmitt was calling
He said the contact person would be a Biff something
I'm thinking Biff? Where do I go with the name Biff?
I mean are we in a cartoon here?
If you could just check the database
Tony, Tim McCurdy here, I'm at La Guardia, been doublechecking
The reason Herman Schmitt was calling
Somebody got their signals semi-crossed
Christine? If you could get back to me
Tony, it turns out Jim Beal is the guy pulling together procedures
as regards the Curly Fries and the GLX-05s
Jim, my office is tracking down the Big Boys contact
Christine? If you could message me at your convenience
You know what? Colonel Stouffer remembered your name
I think I know why—but I digress—more soon
Tony, Tim again, I'm due into Charlotte at 11:20, no wait, that's 12:20
We tracked down the guy in Locksboro, his name is Biff Shaid
S-h-a-i-d but pronounced like Shade
So if you would call Jim Beal at some point
It's about the protocol for this Big Boys package
Christine, what I meant in my previous was strictly something
  complimentary
and hey I appreciate—your focus on all this
This is Tim McCurdy, looking for Mr. Delovega to get back to me

Christine, I'll be in Charlotte at 12:20 and would love to touch base
You'll want to just dovetail with Colonel Stouffer at Fort Bragg
Whatever you can pull together will be helpful
Christine? I haven't heard back from Biff Shaid
I haven't heard back from Tony Delovega
Still no call back from Jim Beal
Just wanted us to be on the same page
You'll want to have all this on your desk when you call Delovega
Jim, it's Tim, the viability is looking good
Herman, thanks again
It's Tim I'm at La Guardia
Tim here
Christine, I know you can get this all on one grid
By the way when I said the Colonel remembered your name
I really meant—you're not someone that someone forgets
Hey, I'm on the ramp now, got to sign off for now
Christine—kind of a question out of left field
Do you ever feel like there's really nothing—
no real reason—
Hey hold that thought Christine, will get back to you in Charlotte—

BONNIE

Standing here in my kitchen at ten past six, a woman not happy,
I could not be more common.

On this same planet today in Darfur
women grab their children and run from the village
to hide among bushes in a ravine because someone said
the janjaweed are riding—one woman runs
trying to carry her baby son and a basket of clothes and bread
and pulling her small wailing daughter by the hand—
into the rocky ravine. They are black and in their desperation
they are important.

I am white and fifty-three and physically safe;
my sandy hair is lightly streaked, my face is freckled;
the fact that I am pale and freckled cooperates with the fact
that I am not important: the two facts go hand in hand.
Scraps of onion peel on my kitchen floor seem gigantic to me
because I am a privileged fool. In my kitchen. I am

a divorced woman who tried, forty minutes ago,
to tempt a younger man to kiss me—to seduce me.
He elected not to. He smiled—kindly—
and left me pale and freckled in my kitchen—palely loitering—
not important—in the scale of things

extremely small—*extremely*. I agree!
I agree. But—I have another thought.
My daughter in her graduation photo on the fridge faces the camera
with such a fragile optimism and staring at her I have this thought:
If I don't matter *at all*—if I am nothing but a pale curdle of silence
in a white kitchen
if I don't even matter *at all*
then nothing matters! Nothing! Not even Darfur. Because—

because the reason why that woman matters terribly
as she runs frantic into the rocky ravine
is because she ought to be free to live like me,
to have her own kitchen with a big refrigerator,
to have a safe life like mine—for what?
So that she could then be—could then be

a human woman Fulfilling Her Human Potential—or what—
her human destiny—her human being. To have the chance.
To see what she can do with the chance.
And so. It follows. There is a logic. If I don't matter *at all*
this evening then it doesn't matter that she can't have what I have
because what would be the point of her surviving if only to be like me
and it won't matter if the janjaweed find her and kill her and her kids.

I hate the fucking janjaweed!

I think all this. I wish
there were someone here to explain it to.

PLOT NOTES

Aunt Emily asks Binx to take Kate to watch a parade
Rheinhardt and Geraldine sing hymns during windstorm at the breakwater
Billy visits Kato on impulse, Kato speaks of the cop she's dating
Wesley meets Wanita and pulls a leech off her leg at the creek

that populated dream is pulsing in your head

Marybeth remembers her conversation with Chuck about Iowa
Marybeth is disturbed by recognition that sometimes people are happy
Mattie cooks dinner for Basil though she senses he has already run off
Mattie thinks Etta is foolish to hope Woods will marry her

you can sleep when you're dead

Kate says she was frighteningly happy after the accident that killed Lyell
Hicks phones his ex-wife Etsuko, she hangs up on him
Geraldine on the bus tries to lie about her scars
Faye dances flirtingly with Miguel, Earl clubs him

it is to wanting that you are wed

Julie arrives, leaves an envelope, takes Chen-yu
Stahr gets a telegram saying Kathleen is married
Ned hears Elaine complaining to Rita about Alec's escapade
Adele says that Ned's disgrace has brought her to life again

that populated dream is pulsing in your head

Byron says Lena knows Brown is a scoundrel but she still wants him
Douglas suddenly arrives in Macon and proposes marriage
Caroline says "I hope I can love you again"
Lucielia tells Mattie that Eugene has straightened out and will stay

it is to wanting that you are wed

Nector swims in the night lake trying to give up Lulu
Lily burns the notebook in which Martha showed her desperation
Martha adopts a pervasive contempt for anyone who desires or loves
Kate arrives by taxi at 3 a.m. exalted by the revelation that each of us is free

you can sleep when you're dead

Fernandez whistles at Cassandra and says his heart demands satisfaction
Lily tolerates the drunk Italian man on the plane
Stahr didn't really love Minna till she was dying
Dot threatens Albertine with a knife, Albertine flings coffee at her

that populated dream keeps on pulsing in your head

Peggy says she has tried to destroy in herself the expectation of happiness
Lena fears she will never see Byron again
Lily wants to be recognized as the princess trapped in the tower
Hicks believes you have to select the worthiest illusion and take a stand

yeah you can sleep when you're dead

Skipper and Miranda chase Jomo and Cassandra in their hot rod
Adele finds the preacher naked in his tent
Elaine lets Freddie seduce her in the car with his "masterful desire"
Joe goes to Bobbie's room unexpectedly and senses she has a man there

everybody hunting for the ultimate bed

Walters chats with Andrew about sex with Flo
Theo feels a mysterious affinity with Marybeth
Mattie rocks Lucielia and Lucielia keens
Culla brings Rinthy an egg and cornbread

that populated dream won't quit pulsing in your head

Hannah imagines Johnny wandering at night by the Canona River
Caroline says "I hope I can love you again"
Hicks believes you select the worthiest illusion and take a stand
Tod thinks of Faye as a bobbing cork, invulnerable
Fernandez tells Cassandra his heart demands satisfaction
Peggy says she has tried to eradicate any hope for happiness
Kate arrives at 3 a.m. exalted by revelation each of us is free
Marybeth gazes across the Bay, imagining escapes

it is to wanting that you are wed
but maybe you can sleep when you're dead

NOT THAT GREAT OF AN EVENING

Yeah I went to the talk, and the reception.
Yeah I went to the dinner, and the party.
It was not a terrible evening. It was okay.
I don't think I did anything especially stupid.
But I feel kind of crummy. Not wretched, you know,
but just kind of lost or left over—
like I'm the little cup of overcooked beans
somebody covered with plastic wrap and pushed to the back of
the fridge. I might drink a little Scotch
just to get sleepy. Everything is okay. But it's like
there's so many voices—all these voices
still skittering around in my head like mice—people
having things to say. Everybody finding lots to say—
this professor gave a talk about the interpenetration
of coexisting cultures—I think that was the concept—
I kind of drifted away in some sections—and then
people clapped so I was clapping and then I was standing
with a cup of wine and trying to have on my face
the I'm-so-interested look. I'm so interested but
I'm also witty and cool. Then I was part of
several little exchanges—not really conversations,
it's more like we're throwing peanuts at each other's mouths.
My peanuts just bounced off the chin or the cheek of
whomever I spoke to. This was partly because the room was so noisy
and my voice is phlegmy and weak. In my next life
I want to have a voice nobody can ignore. But then
I would need to have things to say. Tonight I tried
but I could feel how unriveting I was. I don't blame people
for sliding away from me at the reception, and also at the party.
If I met me tonight I would slide away from me too.

But how do they all *do* it? Are they happy?
I know some of them are not happy, but at least they seem to be so

present. Whereas I was like glancing at the door
waiting for my interesting life to show up.
My cup of wine kept being empty
which made me feel as if I was standing there in my underwear
so I kept refilling it. I was a blur.
I was a blur on its way to becoming a smudge.
And this was not about the evening being terrible. Actually
that's the scary part of it. This was a normal evening
with me being a fuzzy blur. At dinner I kept trying
to look very interested in the conversation on my left or my right
so it wouldn't be obvious that my only true companion was
my plate of salmon and potato. At one point
the troublingly attractive woman across the table was talking
about the talk we heard on coexisting cultures and suddenly
I felt potentially witty and I said loudly, "Who would have thought
that interpenetration could be so boring?" and I grinned at her
and I felt quite rogueish for a quarter of a second
but she just blinked as if I'd thrown a peanut that hit her eyelid
and then she kind of tilted away from me so she could finish her observation
about the ironies of postcolonialism. My face then felt
like a huge decaying pumpkin. Then for a while
I pushed a piece of salmon around on my plate, seeing it as
a postcolonial island, and I imagined the natives muttering
"Things were better under the emperor, at least you knew who you were."

Then after coffee I drifted along to the party upstairs and I thought
there *must* be a way to have fun. What is it?
So I ate three brownies. While nibbling the brownies
I tried to maintain the I'm-so-interested look. I'm sure I chatted
with a dozen people. Several times I started a sentence with
"It's fascinating the way" or "It's so fascinating the way"
but at the moment I can't remember what I was saying was
so fascinating. It was something about memories of high school
at one point. At the party there were at least four women
who seemed very attractive and I just wanted one of them
to give me some big eye contact, that's all,

the kind of gleaming twinkling eye contact that says
"I am intensely aware of your masculine appeal"
but this did not happen, and I began to feel resentful,
I resented the feeling that the focus of the evening,
the focus of existence, was always over *there* or over *there*
and never like *here* where I was standing.

So yeah. It was like that. At some point pretty late
people were telling jokes and I started telling several people
the old long joke whose punch line is,
"Let your pages do the walking through the Yellow Fingers"
but somehow it took forever and only one person really heard the punch line
and he just patted my shoulder and said something like
"Time to get this old steed back to the stable."
Then we both laughed and actually I was happy then
for a second. After that I sat on the sofa
drinking something that looked like wine
and I felt I was such a blur it was like I was the sofa's third cushion.
And then apparently my shoes carried me all the way to this room
where it's just me and the Scotch and the empty bed.
Okay, so not that great of an evening, but no tragedy either;
but I'd just like to feel how it feels to be
in focus at the focus, to feel "Hey, you want the party?
Seek no more! The party's right here."

OLAFUR OF LJOSAVIK

I sit here and read about Olafur Karason of Ljosavik,
a highly sensitive protagonist,
standing on the icy shore of a bay
watching the frigid graygreen waves
crumble in foam and gasp out across the shingle.

Alternatively, I could go to some beach in winter
and stand there having my own sense
of infinity and empty fullness and the world's inscrutability.
There would be one kind of courage in that.

But there is another kind of courage required
for reading about Olafur Karason of Ljosavik
and turning the page to read more
and more about his tribulations on a distant shore
without admitting there is no point
and letting death thus seep into my spine.

(And there are still other kinds of courage with sharper edges
but I feel too misty-bardic just now to consider them.)

THREE FLAWS

Let's say I do succeed, just for the sake of discussion
let's say my writing becomes so incredible
that I'm like unforgettable
and people want everything I ever wrote,
the way people feel about every scrap by Shelley or Keats—
everything, my diaries ever since 1974,
my letters, my notebooks—every letter; every notebook
all preserved, all *kept*—hence not absurd—
my boxes and files not absurd!

Still there would be flaws in the situation.

First, when my body becomes an old man's body
it will still be an old man's body even if
every page I ever wrote is cherished
by vigorous intense younger people
including many sparkling women age 28.

Second, when I die this I here will be, well, obviously,
will be—gone—this I who says "I"—will be
gone—oblivious—obliviated—the one who says "I have won" will
not be.

A reliable remediation of that flaw would be worth several big awards.

When I see my old man's body rolled into a black
mortician's sack my notebooks begin to smell like trash.

Also I detect a third flaw
in the scenario of my triumph
and this one, you'll be surprised to hear, is not only about me.
It's about you. You have interesting notebooks—

I can tell from your eyes that you do;
what will happen to all your interesting notebooks and quirky loose papers
fifty years hence
even if all my own traces are then deathlessly cherished?
Your traces—idiosyncratic notions—Zip disks—
I see them boxed in wet cardboard
in a corner of a blackening garage:
the blackening garage of uncaring futurity!

And as I gaze upon those damp stacked boxes
full of your interesting notebooks and your hopeful manuscripts
waiting to be dumped
I feel—lonely;
I feel isolated in my brilliance; and I can grasp
why you're not thrilled by the prospect of my immense triumph.
So then, do I want you to be tremendously important too?
Well, no, that—that wouldn't make sense—
there's only one apex, one summit, I mean we can't all—
but if your work could be preserved enough to provide
a sort of context, or backdrop… Then my immense triumph
wouldn't have to seem sort of freakish.

So, there are these flaws, one of which involves
your descent toward the dark garage.
Nevertheless I shall continue to strive
(or at least continue to imitate the striving
enough so I can believe it is striving)
because if I don't
then the silence of the hazy summer sky above Chubb Hall
is too blank—too loudly, deafeningly, deafly blank—
as if none of us mattered at all.

TRIP TO VERMONT (ABRIDGED VERSION)

He meant to get a bus from Boston to Vermont
but the bus he boarded was bound for Concord, New Hampshire.
It would take too long to explain why he made this mistake;
it involved his wish to avoid asking clueless questions.
The coat he wore on the bus to Concord was not clean
and it was too heavy for the early spring weather;
it would take too long to say why he wore this coat;
it involved his stubborn rigid loyalty to old clothing,
which reflected his general compulsive loyalty to the past,
particularly his own past, old versions of himself—
a narcissistic devotion to what he was years ago.
The satchel—fake leather—his mother called it a Gladstone bag—
the satchel he carried on the bus was filled with books.
To identify all eighteen of the books would take too long
and to explain why he was carrying these particular books
would take much longer. They were mostly novels
but also a biography of Robespierre and a study of Browning
and two books about the Sioux... Explanation would involve
his refusal, throughout his twenties, to admit
the obvious truth that he could not learn everything
and didn't even really want to. Also, his compulsive wish
to *possess* books regardless of whether he would read them.
In fact he never did read most of those eighteen books.
On the bus he did read some of *Second Skin* by John Hawkes
which made him anxious in ways too complicated to describe fully
involving a certain revulsion against sensuality
(maybe because it undermines identity if identity depends
on the brain's power to order, arrange, configure, control)
and also involving worry about what he could never write.
In Concord he waited an hour—it would take an hour
more or less to report his musings as he wandered
the streets near the bus station—pharmacy, muffler shop—
and then he got a bus to White River Junction;

on that bus he mostly stared out the window
thinking about young women named Becky and Jan.
The essence of his thoughts about Becky and Jan might be
terribly easy to summarize, but there were nuances,
truly hundreds of nuances, far beyond the scope of this account
or any account likely to occur.
The Becky thoughts involved his dishonesty,
and the Jan thoughts involved his cowardice...
From White River Junction he hitchhiked to the town
where his parents owned a house, arriving after dark
in the eeriness of the endless ongoing unreportable.

TO YOU IN 2052

1

I am your forerunner not known to you.
You run not knowing how I ran too.
For I was a limner back when.
In that garish quaint fluxion of documentary confetti strips you call
the past. I was
limner of a yellow house where the talk was of George McGovern
and Carlos Fuentes. A young person crouched by the bookcase
trying to imagine how amazing he might be
if he read all the books by Fuentes. Judy Singsen, not a bad painter,
made an elaborate chicken dish. Pigeons clucked on the sill
near a narrow bed for lovers who listened to Carole King.
A lifetime ago I limned all this! Or some of it, rather.
It was I who did so.

2

You walk on repaved streets
where I imagined transformative successes with long-legged young women
as if you were the first to walk planning what to say to Sally or Sarah;
the lightness of your shoes implies your non-knowing
that I strode there, and limned the longing. The identical longing? Oh
I fear so. But at the time how new. Yes, young blithe one,
I am your forerunner not known to you.
On those same streets I was limner of Bob Pierce and Laird Holby
who played squash at Marvel Gym and walked home pleasantly sweaty
in winter damp on Elmgrove Avenue discussing Watergate, back when.
Each of us trying to figure what a self would feel like.
Thin paychecks had we and vague big futures.

3

And the mailbox after midnight outside a giant pharmacy on East
        Genesee Street
where freedom was absurdly excessive
in the stupid darkness of cars and cars—
that was I standing at that mailbox trying to believe
each letter dropped in was a building block, a forward step;
but with freedom so absurdly empty on East Genesee
it might be necessary to write deceivingly to a young woman
and cause her to climb my stairs
in a pathetically pretty stiff green dress—
then try to limn it all, to limn her limbs, her body
and her loneliness and mine and our clumsy Night Moves—
in some notebook you are not going to hunt for.

4

And later, my son as a Phillies pitcher making ten pickoff moves in a row
to first base which was a lamp in our living room
where the crucial new song was Dylan's "Shooting Star"
and later my daughter in another house whirling and jumping
in order to dramatize a Mozart quartet—
have you heard of Mozart? He made music once.
I'm saying, so much
was lived by me, and limned by me—long back, long gone
but if Thomas Hardy was right about ghosts I'm still very active
in ten houses and on a hundred streets!
Meanwhile now you ride around the same towns
in your lonely arrogance thinking "None of *this* has ever been said."
And I envy you that pleasure. And I hope
that in some sense you're right.

DOWN HERE

We tried being together; after a while it felt like a mistake.

We sat in her kitchen. She said,
"I know that poetry can be very interesting
and I know it makes some people happy and that's fine
but what I can't relate to, in the end,
is the whole thing of plucking something *out* of *life*,
the idea of removing some little piece of life
from the whole messy flow of everything—
the way you think you need to sort of isolate this one bit of experience
in this sort of glass box that you call a poem—
you want to put it in the box
and hoist the box to a top shelf way up
where grubby time won't smudge it—
time with its grubby money and plastic bags of garbage
and people who say they care about you and then don't
and skin fungus and gum decay and arthritis
and car engines breaking down and hospital rooms
and people getting addicted to things—
you think you can put even anybody's mother with Alzheimer's
or anybody's uncle with diabetes or any other piece of the world
into the crystal box if you just trim it to fit—"

(I could see from her face that she liked her metaphor
of the crystal box on the high shelf
and she hoped it was a good enough metaphor
so that I would remember it and remember her for it)

"—and what I can't relate to is the whole assumption
that you can do that and then things are somehow all better
when actually they're not because actually there *is* no top shelf,
I mean everything is *down here* and everything dies.
The poems you're always poking at are pieces of paper

that end up in boxes—*cardboard* boxes—
and the boxes eventually get hauled to a dumpster
by the teenage boys working for your granddaughter's landlord
or the teenage boys helping to clear out a warehouse or a library basement
maybe thirty years from now, maybe sixty, and they end up as landfill
just like you and me and all our friends, we're all on our way
to being landfill—and what we really need
is for each of us to be decent to each other and if possible
to be generous and kind. And those words are boring to you—"

(her voice was now trembling and she was striving not to cry
and I almost realized I was glad to be important enough
to make her nearly cry about this)

"—which is why what I'm saying is not a poem.
Which is why poems are not what I care about because
to me what counts is for people to notice how other people are feeling
and to respond to that *right then* and for people to give each other
little surprise presents and to phone someone and say 'How are you doing'
in a real way and to talk to people about what matters to them
outside your own little world of crystal treasures.
That's what I look for in a person and what happens is,
we do our best and ultimately a few people visit us in the hospital
and then we die."

She stopped and looked away and calmed her breathing.

I thought: I respect her; but I don't think I can love her.
Or, not romantically. And I thought how much worse I would feel
if she had said all this without getting upset.

(She had a way of rapidly tapping her cheekbone with one finger
to keep back tears when she thought tears would be sentimental;
I remembered loving her for that; I saw
how someone else could love that soon.)

I looked down
I gazed down
Down I gazed
Down gazed I into my cold cup of tea.

ANOTHER POINT

People say about Jabez Legend that he was sort of a jerk
with possibly a skin fungus problem due to questionable hygiene
and some bounced checks due to disorganized finances
and many quasi-friends developed reasons not to sit with him
in the Melrose Diner and there is probably a modicum of truth
to all this but is that really what we want to talk about?
I mean let's keep a perspective. We are talking about the guy
who sat up very late one night in that town,
right there in that cramped and grease-specked apartment
on South Drumlin Street with a view of the dumpsters behind Shoney's
and he composed the song "Lament for Lorna". Not just, you know,
another version of "Barefoot Blues" but "Lament for Lorna".
He did it! The song must have been waiting inside him,
a part of him all through whatever else he did or didn't do
that summer in that town of cooked asphalt—
the song waited and then out it came pouring
into the space of the core of that one night;

and I just have to keep thinking how
all those sweaty days he might have *seemed* just, you know,
"some guy" mixing bourbon and Pepsi, "some guy with a guitar"
on hot nights when everybody's mind was on
just pizza and chicken wings and Red Dog beer
in that town which you could call "just a town"
and yet *in reality*—I'm saying the truth is
he wrote "Lament for Lorna". The guitar was there
and the notes were there waiting on any piano
but nobody else found them! That is a reality to keep in mind

when somebody says for example that Jabez Legend lost his job
for stealing stuff at the delicatessen that same week.
Which could be true or not, and somebody else has said
he was not trustworthy with a woman named Nancy

that same summer, supposedly he messed with her mind
in some disrespectful fashion and that is possibly
accurate as far as it goes but what I am saying—

my point is another point. My point is, hey,
who wrote "Lament for Lorna"? He did!
He took the pizza and the beer and the asphalt
and the sound of voices from a party a block away
and the stupidity on TV and the glow of the all-night Shell station
and a memory of some girl glancing out of a window
and he metamorphosed all that
into something else
which is "Lament for Lorna".
The middle part in that song—on the record it's just
a single violin—that part kills me. Which is to say
it puts me in another life. It takes my heart
and empties out some dark pool of trouble
and leaves my heart dry and quiet on a hillside
and the name of that hillside is Acceptance.
And I just want to say
that to be the guy who wrote that song
might not change whatever else he was
but whatever else he was *was*
whereas that song *is*, man, that song *exists*.
"Lament for Lorna."
Unlike me and you, and unlike Jabez too
and unlike all the real-life human stuff we do
that song is not going away.

JULIE AT THE READING

He stands up there reading us his story
all about this guy who can't stop thinking about sex
and how he goes after this younger woman
even though he's married to a social worker
and how he wants to get the younger woman drunk
and unzip her blue dress while his wife is out of town
and we get this comical exaggerated paragraph about the unzipping
which does happen because she thinks he is so witty
though first they have all these amusing worries and doubts
all over town but then they do it in her tiny apartment
while a Hank Williams record plays and I love Hank Williams
because his voice is the opposite of pretending
which is why he did not belong in this story
and there's a sentence about glowing skin, how their skin glows
and then at the end he's all Beautifully Confused

and we just sit and listen and we understand
that it's all about expressing the reality of human desires
because we need to face the wild elements of our nature
and literature gives us a safe place to do this

and then we applaud him and then there's the reception
with wine and little chunks of cheese
and everybody just sort of chats pleasantly
like "We enjoyed it so much, it was such a funny story"
and "Do you like write every day or only when you're inspired?"
Because we understand the story wasn't really *true*
the way life is true because if it was

then I think we would be thinking about his wife in real life
and how does *she* feel about him expressing the reality of human desires,
and what is the promise that a man makes

when he pushes so far deep inside you
and what is a promise at all anyway
and how does that woman with the blue dress feel
the day after the sexy story with her cold Defenders of Wildlife coffee mug
and we would ask him some real questions
instead of just nibbling cheese and telling him
how funny his descriptions were.

CLOUD OF LUCK

Because I have lived almost uninterruptedly in a cloud of luck

(but my mother died of cancer thirty years ago,
so mauled internally and exhausted in her last months
she could barely turn her head on the pillow
to attempt an impossible faraway smile)

my poems have had to be mainly
poems from a cloud of luck
(fabulously far from Abu Ghraib
as from anything metaphorically like Abu Ghraib)

and I ask the blind and deaf and brainless Powers
to let this continue for thirty more years at least
and if the price of this is that I must be a minor poet
(though I would theoretically question such inevitability)
then
I accept the price—I embrace it!
Where do I sign?

(Note to self: omit this one.
Too vulnrbl—why give such easy ammo to hostile reviewers?
Anyway, need reflect more on diff betw outward luck
& psych/emo luck. Also
mother's death invoked oft before. Also
Abu Ghraib ref too newsy contempo. Also
nothing really *done* w. cloud metaph.
Also need think thru correlation or noncorr
betw misery & majorness—topic
more appro for essay. Also
maybe dangerous attract atten of Fates? Omit.)

AGONIST

He is sculpting a giant statue of himself

ostensibly to express the crucifixal frustrations of us all
with our vast spirits stapled to contingency and incompleteness
he chisels, hammers, welds, polishes—every day

even when he might appear to be merely going to a restaurant
you are to understand that he never lapses from his commitment
which throbs on behind roast duck in orange sauce

to sculpt his giant statue—of himself...

But isn't it really for us? Isn't it THE SELF straining up
against the time-shackles and flesh-cords binding us all?
Oh sure it is, though what moves him intently to his hard tools
is how the marbly figure glows of *him* for *him*...

Before dawn he frowns in the solitude of creation
soldering more dark gemstones into the edifice:
harsh brave metaphors riveted welded pounded *whack*

and it goes on all day as along the rainswept leaf-strewn sidewalk
he carries all humanity's intolerable hunger
toward another restaurant

where he will articulate distinctions between his own excruciated sculpting
and that of Cavafy or Rilke or Celan or Yeats.

Outrage and anguish are not messy muddly Daily News things—
they are fierce sharp marbly things suitable for gigantic sculpture

in the chisel-bright studio of agonism after the restaurant
where he keeps sculpting (ostensibly on behalf of us all)
a statue of himself

and some people downtown are primed to tell him it is VERY tall.

ENCHANTED FIELD

I am being given my chance
and I am blowing it. I am under a spell
whereby I have no choice but to waste my chance.

This sun-dapply morning I feel my vast chance being poured out upon me
but I am too stupid to grasp or even identify what it is…
But it must have something to do with what is here—

what is in my hand? It is a novella by Henry James.
I could be standing, moving, helping to build a house for the poor,
cooking lamb in spinach sauce—instead
I sit here with Henry James. I think this is the tenth James book I've read!
At one level I'm proud of this but on another level this seems
a grotesquely vivid picture of me blowing my chance.
How much Jamesian nuance should a person savor in one life on earth?
To see in words precisely how the sisters of Gaston Probert deal
with the embarrassment of his infatuation
with a rich but unsophisticated American girl, Francie Dosson—

Francie's beauty is as clear and impenetrable as a pine grove across a valley.
Across a valley… Trees whisper outside; traffic whirs;
men are out there burying cables;
women ride away on motorinos—past churches full of dark paintings.
Upon the million roofs, sunshine—my chance…

This is the kingdom of the missing of the chance:
paradise lost all day; Milton, how to be living enough at this hour?
Now in the radiating complexity of what is missed
I notice my daughter who in her Teletubbies peejays
earnestly on the sunny floor works at her new drawing;
she tells me its title with great assurance: "Enchanted Field."

ASK WENDY WISDOM

Dear Wendy Wisdom,

My second marriage ended a few years ago. My daughter graduated from college
this year. Lately I feel lost. I keep thinking there's someone I could meet
who would make my life exciting and important.
But when I have dinner with friends of friends,
the restaurant roars like a wind-tunnel of mutual boredom.
I keep using Google to locate people I dated, or had crushes on,
twenty or thirty years ago. But of course they turn out to have spouses, kids, lives,
they don't feel a craving to reconnect with me—only a brief curiosity.
Their e-mails say "How nice to hear from you"—but their messages get
shorter and shorter; the fourth message is nothing but
"Hope things work out!" In coffeeshops I see attractive individuals;
I think I sometimes stare at them too long. Once or twice
I've followed someone along a snowswept sidewalk
trying to think of something to say—"Would you like another decaf mocha?"
I feel invisible. I feel like a coat on a second-hand rack. I feel
like wet snow clinging to the side of a mail truck. What do you suggest?

—Mopey in Minneapolis

Dear Mopey,

First of all, moping is extremely unattractive.
The only reliable way to make oneself attractive is through
sustained intense interest in some subject (other than romance and sex).
Sustained intense interest is impossible to fake. Meanwhile,
you need to consider that relationship with another actual person
may not be able to give you the sense of visibility, significance, importance
you long for. Certainly if the idea of relationship is for you
essentially a conduit toward orgasm, your quest is doomed

by its objective. Orgasm is terribly overrated. It is chemically addictive,
but like other drugs it betrays you and leaves you grimacing in the
       bathroom.
If orgasm is what your daydreams basically hanker toward,
the only cure is old age—if that. Meanwhile,
it's true there are probably persons in the world with whom you could have
a fabulously meaningful and fulfilling friendship. Think of Emma
       Thompson
as she seems—the real-person equivalent of Emma Thompson probably
       does exist
within twenty miles of where you live in Minneapolis. But
you are very unlikely to find her. Therefore
what I suggest to you is: *representation*. Create
representations of your loneliness, your lostness, your boredom, your
       moping.
You seem to be good with words, so do your representing in words.
Represent the ice-crusted streets, the streetlights seen through wet
       windshields,
the vapid conversations about the Vikings and college tuition fees and sitcoms
and the brevity of years, also represent the alarming streaks of intelligence
that appear in some conversations, also the ponytailed waitress
whose smile complicates her expert curtness and whom you overhear
telling a waiter "I'm still living with Ashley and Kristie
because when I'm alone I just cry all the time." Represent
all this in great detail. Also represent the experiences, encounters
you wish could happen—with fierce attention to detail.
Elaborate your representations so richly that a reader can virtually live
       in them!
Then let that reader be your dear companion.
Imagine that reader sitting thoughtfully beside a lamp on the far side of
       the room.

                                                —Wisely yours,
                                                Wendy Wisdom

SOUTH OF MORGANTOWN

In the other day of the other life in a space south of Morgantown
it goes on. It continues there;
you can't see the kids but their voices float like a spray
up through the pines. Those hundreds of pines all so calm,
studying how to get some sun and rain in useful amounts
for getting tall and what else, taller and expressing
boughs outward every way. This continues there
south of Morgantown and on a hot day
all the kids go over to Lake Floyd
along about three p.m. They ride down Flinderation Road
and they drink some Pepsi or beer depending on their age
and jump around in Lake Floyd a while
and dry off on the rocks, maybe play cards.

                                                                     We feel
a stretching in ourselves toward them, those kids down there
or is it toward the lake itself or toward the calm of those pine trees
because our life, this one, seems like what happens when
the fine clear simple thing is somewhere else. Those kids ride
far down Flinderation Road out of sight and when their voices come
like spindrift of hot haze the force of it is the way we don't see them,
we don't see the sweat on the freckles, the dirt in the sweat,
the blue bubble gum and the fatuous small cruelties or
blind enforcements of loneliness; and so they can be
in that other day down there the sense of what clear fine thing
we've failed to keep.
                                Anne, Anne,
sit near me on the rock while we dry in the sun.
Anne, those droplets on your legs are shining so quietly!
What is the song she hums as if to herself but letting us hear?
It is "Dream a Little Dream of Me."

GUIDEBOOK EMBARRASSMENT

What I saw—what I now think I saw
was the Madonna della Mela by Luca della Robbia
and the Madonna Panciatichi by Desiderio da Settignano
and the Bacchus With Pard by Jacopo Sansovino—
but I was on the wrong page of the guidebook—
and so I missed the full effect—what I got
was an itchy fuzzy kind of feeling; because,
what I thought I was seeing was
the Birth of Jesus by Antonio Pollaiolo
and the Bust of a Woman With a Cornucopia by Tino di Camaino
and the Decapitation by Andrea del Verrocchio—

or else, for a minute I also considered
that these all might be Scenes From the Life of Saint Zanobi.
The guidebook was confusing, and the museum was jammed,
and my lower back started creaking the way it does.
So when I emerged my whole sensation was woolly,
as if the museum visit happened ten years ago
and melded and merged across the years with several other museums
and several other guidebooks and someone's Renaissance calendar.
In the piazza I stood frowning. Sunshine hit the guidebook
so the pages were only white glare. Someone said

Wasn't the art incredible, and I didn't want to seem like
just a woolly donkey oblivious of our marvelous Western heritage
so I said I kind of liked the Birth of Jesus by Pollaiolo
though I missed the three kings.
To this, people replied "Uh huh" sort of neutrally.
I said I wasn't so keen on the Decapitation by Verrocchio
because (I observed humorously) "You couldn't even tell
whose head was going to be chopped off." People glanced at me
sideways when I said this. I began to sense
that I'd missed the right experience,

my experience had been wrong or maybe
not an experience at all. And now I just wanted lunch,

I wanted to sit down in a pizzeria with smooth tablecloths
and talk about ravioli instead of art. Sometimes
you might by mistake order the wrong kind of ravioli
but it wouldn't mean you were missing
some key to the profound meaning of civilization.
If you want ravioli stuffed with carciofi
and you get ravioli stuffed with funghi
this is just a funny little surprise and maybe a happy adventure.
If the menu is confusing, it's still just a menu.
But when the guidebook is confusing,

you stare at the Madonna della Mela by Luca della Robbia
and you try to think Ah this is an interesting interpretation
of the Birth of Jesus, by Antonio Pollaiolo, with no Nativity scene,
and the Mela must metaphorically represent the gifts of the Magi,
and you stare at the Madonna Panciatichi by Desiderio da Settignano
and you try to think Ah this is how Tino di Camaino
represented the abundance of life, so in a sense
her belly must be the cornucopia, along with her bust.
And you stare at a Bacchus whose head is not off
and you try to think Okay I guess too much wine
does in a way kind of decapitate a person
and maybe that big cat there is just about to do something terrible?
You try to think sensitively like this,
but the sensitive thoughts are not sticking to the great art

because it's the wrong great art
and the itch-fuzz feeling starts
and the names Tino di Camaino and Antonio Pollaiolo and Andrea
    del Verrocchio
sound suspiciously like nothing but antique boxes of syllables.
Standing in the sweaty piazza I just hated that whole Italian circus
for being nothing but a cornucopia of gaudy noise
without a good guidebook, and hated myself for believing

the guidebook could make it all Marvelous and Inspiring
if you just found the correct page—

and I didn't cheer up till we got to Ristorante Cellini
and I studied eggplant parmigiana with vino rosso:
Let's see, which of these is the food and which is the drink?
Not a puzzle! And I felt sure
that even in the Life of old Saint Zanobi there were scenes
that had a lot more to do with melanzane and vino
than with Virgin Birth and Decapitation and haloes.
A *lot* more...
                              But then after the tiramisu
which was fairly good but a bit too heavy
we left the Cellini and walked
through the open-air market
where the eyes of the piled fish said:

We were helpless mechanisms of hunger
flushed into the green dark glut of the world
and scooped out of it
to lie stacked mindless on cubes of ice

and by the time we got to the hotel I was vaguely thinking
there must be some proof that we are DEEPLY
different from the market's catch of the day
and I thought: Tomorrow I will buy a new guidebook,
a big one that is very clear.

WAY WAY UP THERE

At the top of the Milky Way
there is a room where sits the Narrator Supreme
filling thickest of notebooks
with the total story of everything that has ever mattered—

in that dark scrawl Rome is set down,
and Carthage, I, you, all,
preserving detail with fanatical devotion,

including whatever went wrong between your sister and someone else
in 1999, a year of many rooms with doors opening into the jungle,
and whatever went wrong between me and Chris Savard
after our hilarious late-night ping pong games in 1968
and the haunting nonconnection between me and Maggie
after we danced to Toots and the Maytals in 1974
and whatever happened to that sweet boy Carl
who liked to go with us to Nifty Fifty's in 1993
across a landscape of broken windows and pillaged payphones

—and all the confusion and folly and failure
pass through a cool registration
into gentle comedy and then
into a sober forgiveness and then
into a quiet condition of being eternally respected
without loss of minute figuration.

(Or so I say
because I need to say so
for the feeling of the saying
but the hand of the NS may sometimes get tired
so just in case
we try to note what's notable in our hot dot of space.)

Find These Uncommonly Good Tupelo Press Books
at tupelopress.org or call 802-366-8185

On Dream Street	(2007)	Melanie Almeder	$16.95
The Animal Gospels	(2006)	Brian Barker	$16.95
The Gathering Eye	(2004)	Tina Barr	$14.95
Mulberry	(2006)	Dan Beachy-Quick	$16.95
Bellini in Istanbul	(2005)	Lillias Bever	$16.95
Cloisters	(2008)	Kristin Bock	$16.95
Sincerest Flatteries	(2007)	Kurt Brown	$ 9.95
Modern History, Prose Poems 1987-2007	(2008)	Christopher Buckley	$16.95
After the Gold Rush	(2006)	Lewis Buzbee	$14.00
The Flammable Bird	(2006)	Elena Karina Byrne	$14.95
Masque	(2007)	Elena Karina Byrne	$16.95
Spill	(2007)	Michael Chitwood	$16.95
Signed, numbered limited edition hardcover*			$100.00
Locket	(2005)	Catherine Daly	$16.95
Psalm	(2007)	Carol Ann Davis	$16.95
Signed, numbered limited edition hardcover*			$100.00
The Flute Ship "Castricum"	(2001)	Amy England	$14.95
Victory & Her Opposites	(2007)	Amy England	$19.95
Duties of the Spirit	(2005)	Patricia Fargnoli	$16.95
Calendars	(2003)	Annie Finch	$14.95 (pb) $22.95 (hc)
Ice, Mouth, Song	(2005)	Rachel Contreni Flynn	$16.95
Mating Season	(2004)	Kate Gale	$16.95
Do The Math	(2008)	Emily Galvin	$16.95
Other Fugitives and Other Strangers	(2006)	Rigoberto Gonzalez	$16.95
No Boundaries	(2003)	Ray Gonzalez, ed.	$22.95
Time Lapse	(2003)	Alvin Greenberg	$22.95 (hc)
Keep This Forever	(2008)	Mark Halliday	$16.95 (pb) $21.95 (hc)
Longing Distance	(2004)	Sarah Hannah	$16.95
Inflorescence	(2007)	Sarah Hannah	$16.95
Numbered limited edition hardcover*			$100.00
Invitaion to a Secret Feast	(2008)	Joumana Haddad	$16.95
Night, Fish, and Charlie Parker	(2006)	Phan Nhien Hao	$16.95
The Next Ancient World	(2001)	Jennifer Michael Hecht	$13.95
A House Waiting for Music	(2003)	David Hernandez	$14.95
Storm Damage	(2002)	Melissa Hotchkiss	$13.95
Red Summer	(2006)	Amaud Jamaul Johnson	$16.95
Dancing in Odessa	(2004)	Ilya Kaminsky	$16.95
The Garden Room	(2006)	Joy Katz	$ 9.95

Abiding Places, Korea North and South	(2006)	Ko Un	$16.95
You Can Tell the Horse Anything	(2004)	Mary Koncel	$14.95
Ardor	(2008)	Karen An Hwei Lee	$16.95
Dismal Rock	(2007)	Davis McCombs	$16.95
Signed, numbered limited edition hardcover*			$100.00
Biogeography	(2008)	Sandra Meek	$16.95
Bright Turquoise Umbrella	(2004)	Hermine Meinhard	$16.95
Why is the Edge Always Windy?	(2005)	Mong Lan	$16.95
Vacationland	(2005)	Ander Monson	$16.95
Miracle Fruit	(2003)	Aimee Nezhukumatathil	$14.95
At the Drive-In Volcano	(2007)	Aimee Nezhukumatathil	$16.95
The Imaginary Poets	(2005)	Alan Michael Parker, ed.	$19.95
Everyone Coming Toward You	(2005)	David Petruzelli	$16.95
Darkling	(2001)	Anna Rabinowitz	$14.95
The Wanton Sublime	(2006)	Anna Rabinowitz	$16.95
When the Eye Forms	(2006)	Dwaine Rieves	$16.95
Bend	(2004)	Natasha Sajé	$14.95
Approximately Paradise	(2005)	Floyd Skloot	$16.95
Selected Poems: 1970-2005	(2008)	Floyd Skloot	$17.95
Distant Early Warning	(2005)	Rad Smith	$16.95
O Woolly City	(2007)	Priscilla Sneff	$16.95
Every Bird is One Bird	(2001)	Francine Sterle	$13.95
Nude in Winter	(2006)	Francine Sterle	$16.95
Embyros & Idiots	(2007)	Larissa Szporluk	$16.95
I Want This World	(2001)	Margaret Szumowski	$13.95
The Night of the Lunar Eclipse	(2005)	Margaret Szumowski	$16.95
In the Mynah Bird's Own Words	(2002)	Barbara Tran	$9.95
Devoted Creatures	(2004)	Bill Van Every	$14.95
This Sharpening	(2006)	Ellen Doré Watson	$16.95
The Way Home, A Wilderness Odyssey	(2004)	Bibi Wein	$16.95
Narcissus	(2008)	Cecilia Woloch	$ 9.95
The Making of Collateral Beauty	(2006)	Mark Yakich	$ 9.95
American Linden	(2002)	Matthew Zapruder	$14.95 (pb) $22.95 (hc)

* Proceeds from the purchase of these limited edition books help to support
Poetry in the Schools, a national initiative that brings working poets into elementary
and high schools across the country.